CODE R.E.D.:

Activate Your Purpose

PAMELA KNIGHT, Ph.D.

PDK PUBLISHING, LLC

TABLE OF CONTENTS

ACKNOWLEDGMENTS

I want to say a special "Thank You" to my mom, Shirley Knight! She has always loved and supported me unconditionally, and I couldn't ask for a better mother.

In loving memory of my father, Joe Knight, words cannot express how much you're missed. Although you're not here with me physically, I know that you're watching over me.

To all of my family and friends, thank you so much for all of your love and support. I'm so blessed to have you all in my life.

PURPOSE

C ODE R.E.D. is a book designed to sound the alarm and jumpstart your process to becoming your true, authentic self so that you can activate your purpose. Your true authentic self is the person you keep hidden from everyone, maybe even yourself. The authentic self is often hidden for a variety of reasons. Life happens, and as a result of life, we experience life stressors, such as mental/physical conditions, trauma, grief, etc. At some point on this journey called life, we learned that it hurts to be rejected or not accepted for who we are. Therefore, we bury our authentic selves as a form of protecting ourselves from others and from life. In the process of burying our authentic selves, we delay our development and growth into the person that we are destined to be in life. The longer we delay our development and growth, the longer it takes for us to activate our purpose. CODE R.E.D. will guide you through the process of self-discovery and activating your purpose. The acronym **RED** stands for: **R**ecognize the issue, **E**nvision your dream, and **D**are to be your authentic self.

This book is written from a biblical perspective. Therefore, scriptures and biblical examples are utilized throughout the chapters of this book. For those of you who do not subscribe to Christianity, do not let this keep you from learning how to push past your affliction to become your true, authentic self and activate your purpose.

Recognize
The Issue

AFFLICTION

"Although the Lord gives you the bread of adversity
and the water of affliction, your teachers will be
hidden no more; with your own eyes you will see
them. Whether you turn to the right or to the left, your
ears will hear a voice behind you, saying, "This is the
way; walk in it."

Isaiah 30: 20 – 21 (NIV)

F or the purposes of this book, let's define affliction as whatever condition that stunts your growth and development and hinders you from moving into your purpose. It can be medical/physical, mental/emotional, or spiritual. We **ALL** have some sort of affliction in our lives. The difference between you and I may be how we handle that affliction. With that in mind, let's examine your perspective on your affliction. How do you see your affliction? How much power and influence have you given to your affliction?

Is your affliction hindering you from becoming your true, authentic self and activating your purpose? Activating your purpose requires you to face your affliction. Therefore, affliction is essential to the activation process. In

> "Activating your purpose requires you to face your affliction."

order to activate your purpose, you must first endure the process of self-discovery. So, what do I mean by that? When you face your affliction, your outcome as far as who you are is different from the person you were when you first started to face your affliction. Your affliction often educates you, stretches you, develops your critical thinking skills, and causes you to face many of your fears that you were unaware of at the time. You can't avoid it. You can't prevent it. You can't discard it. You have to face your affliction. Whether or not you are victorious over your affliction is up to you. It depends on how you view your affliction.

Many of us tend to give our affliction more power and influence over our lives than it deserves. Rather than challenging the affliction, we give it full reign for fear of the outcome from confronting our affliction. Some people get so tired of challenging the affliction that it's just easier to give up and allow affliction to have full reign. Affliction then becomes bigger and more of an obstacle for us. I need you to see this. The affliction that you are suffering with did not become bigger and more challenging on its own. It received your help by your willingness to relinquish your control and power over to it. Sometimes the size of your affliction is what you make it. It's all about our perception of the affliction. We always look for someone to blame for our affliction. Did I do something wrong? If he/she had not done this, I would not have

> "The size of your affliction is what you make it."

to go through this. Here's a question that often boggles the mind. Why is God doing this to me? This question has been the cause of so many strained relationships with God. Now . . . I know God is our Creator, and He knows all things. What if He is not the cause of your affliction? What if God allows the affliction in an effort to stretch you so that you can walk into your purpose? The fact is, God cannot bless you with what He has intended for you until you have developed and grown into the person who is capable of handling that blessing. What do I mean by that? The person you were at the beginning of your journey will not be the person you are towards the end of your journey. What do you think would happen if God blessed you with everything you asked for when you asked for it? You would not be in the mindset to appreciate it or do what it

> "There must be a time of preparation so that you will be of the right mindset to handle what God has in store for you."

takes to maintain it. For example, God could have blessed you with millions of dollars in your twenties. However, you may have squandered that money or spent that money impulsively because it was given to you. You didn't earn it. Therefore, there must be a time of preparation so that you will be of the right mindset to handle what God has in store for you. See . . . you may have to go through a period of time when you experience what it is like to have a limited amount of money. Have you ever gone through times when you didn't know how you were going to pay your mortgage/rent or car note? Have you ever gone through a time when you had to rob Peter to pay Paul? Have you ever lost a job and did not have enough savings to help you get through the next month? These trials and tribulations are a part of your training process. Due to these trials and tribulations, you learned how to budget your money. You learned how to discipline yourself in regard to spending. You learned the importance of saving for a rainy day. You learned the importance of generational wealth. Now don't get me wrong, sometimes the trials and tribulations are more complicated than the example provided. Although the rationale for why people experience the trials and tribulations they go through may never be understood, you never know if your journey is attached to the lifeline of someone else. Your testimony may be the difference between life and death for someone else. Never discount your experience because it molds you into the person that is capable of handling God's purpose for your life.

FEAR

*"For God has not given us a spirit of fear, but of
power and of love and of a sound mind."*

2 Timothy 1: 7 (NKJV)

F ear is often introduced into our lives as a result of our experience with our affliction(s). It is often fear that paralyzes us from moving forward in our purpose. It's hard to face the unknown. It's hard to put yourself out there for others to see. It's difficult to acknowledge that you are afraid, period. With that being said, I want to share another perspective with you on fear. I want to talk to you about fear in the context of being in relationship with fear. You may be wondering the reason I want to take this approach. Well, it's simple. It's hard to discuss or examine fear when you have a hard time acknowledging it in the first place. If you're reluctant to even acknowledge that you are afraid in the first place, then how are you going to address your fears? Fear has a significant impact on you, your relationships, achieving your dreams/goals, and activating your purpose. As an example of how fear impacts your relationships, let's examine how fear interferes with your relationship with God.

Now some of you may wonder what fear has to do with being in a relationship with God. Fear can fashion itself in many forms in our lives, such as depression, anxiety, anger, unforgiveness, rejection, paranoia, and many others. When you think about God, is He about any of these things I mentioned? No. Therefore, fear can act as a hindrance to your relationship with God. So, for the purpose of this chapter, let's consider fear to be the enemy. You know who the enemy is, right? The one who does not want you to have a close relationship with God. That's right . . . him. So, what does the enemy come to do?

> "The enemy comes to steal your hope, kill your dreams, and destroy God's purpose for your life."

According to John 10:10 (KJV), the enemy comes to "steal, kill, and destroy." What does the enemy come to steal, kill, and destroy? He comes to steal your hope. He comes to kill your dreams. He comes to destroy God's purpose for your life. In essence, he comes to kill, steal, and destroy your faith and relationship with God. In order for the enemy to fulfill his purpose, he begins to plant seeds of doubt. As a result of allowing fear to influence us, we begin to change our perspective on who we are, how we perceive ourselves to be, and who God is to us. Therefore, we become distracted from building a relationship with God and begin to build a relationship with fear.

Let's think about that for a minute. Instead of focusing on building a relationship with God, you begin to focus on building a relationship with fear. Why? We don't even have the answer to that question, but that's what we do. Fear inserts itself in our lives and tells us that we need it. It whispers words of doubt in our minds and spirit as if it is looking out for us. As a result, fear stunts our growth and prevents us from moving forward towards our full potential. Think about it. How many times have you heard an inner voice in your head telling you that you can't do that . . . you can't get that promotion, you can't start your own business, you're not good enough, or you're not pretty enough. As a result of listening to that inner voice, we don't take the necessary steps to move forward in our lives. We don't apply for that job. We don't start that business. We don't pursue that relationship. Therefore, we become stuck and begin to ask ourselves why we are not moving forward. We then look to God and wonder why He is not blessing us like He's blessing others. However, we are not in a relationship with God but in a relationship with fear. When you think about being in a relationship with someone, should that relationship build you up or tear you down? If your response is that a relationship should build you up and encourage you to be your best self, then you may need to re-evaluate your relationship with fear if it's not that type of relationship. Is your relationship with fear healthy, unhealthy, or both?

How do you determine whether or not your relationship with fear is healthy, unhealthy, or both? In order to determine whether or not you have a healthy or unhealthy relationship with fear, you must do a little self-reflection. There are a couple of exercises provided below to assist you in determining whether or not your relationship with fear is healthy or unhealthy.

Exercise 1:

Please list how your fear hinders you.

_____   _____

_____   _____

_____   _____

_____   _____

_____   _____

Just take a minute to examine this list. When you look at this list, how does it make you feel? What is going through your head as you read over your list? Are you happy with how your fear hinders you?

The following exercise may seem a little strange, but please keep an open mind. The following exercise requires you to list how fear benefits you. Before you just dismiss this, know that this step is crucial to this process. Remember, self-reflection isn't easy.

> "Self-reflection isn't easy."

Exercise 2:

Please list how your fear benefits you.

_____   _____

_____   _____

_____   _____

_____   _____

_____   _____

As you review this list, I really want you to think about it. We often stay in relationships that are unhealthy for us for a reason. Although the relationship may be unhealthy, the relationship fulfills a need within us. Let's think about it. What need did your fear fulfill within you? For example, your fear may have provided you with a sense of protection from fear of the unknown. See . . . it's harder to step out on faith and trust that everything will be okay. At least we know where we stand if we remain in this relationship with fear, right? Now, revisit the list of how your fear benefits you. If we are going to determine if your relationship with fear is unhealthy or healthy, we have to examine the relationship from all angles. Based on your review of both lists, is your relationship with fear unhealthy, healthy, or both?

If you determine that your relationship with fear is unhealthy, what needs to happen? Think back to a relationship with an old boyfriend/girlfriend. At some point in the relationship, you realized that the relationship was unhealthy or was not working out. What did you do? Some people might remain in the relationship even though it was unhealthy due to the fact that the relationship fulfilled a need in their life, such as companionship. Those people fear being alone. Some people choose to separate themselves from the other person due to the fact that the relationship is more of a hindrance than a help.

If you determine that your relationship with fear is healthy, what needs to happen? This is the person whose benefits outweigh the hindrances. Fear may serve more as a motivator for you or challenges you to be your best self and to walk into your full potential. It doesn't mean that there are no challenges, but you have learned to manage your fear well.

If you determine that your relationship with fear is both unhealthy and healthy, what needs to happen? Well, you need to find a balance. In your life, fear may hinder you from being your authentic self and hinder you from moving forward. However, there are times in which you need that fear. For example, anxiety may hinder you from taking steps to apply for a job or to start your business. On the flip side, anxiety may serve as a benefit to you if you are impulsive with your spending. The anxiety might cause you to pause and think about the fact that you need to have enough money to pay your rent/mortgage, utilities, food, and any other bills that are generated during the month.

Okay, so you have determined the type of relationship you have with fear. Great. We are not quite finished. Depending on your relationship with fear, you have to learn how to challenge fear or manage it. Sometimes, fear plays such a significant part in our lives that we become one with fear. We actually take on the identity of our fear. We are depression. We are rejected. We are not good enough. We are unforgiving. In an effort to challenge and/or manage

> "In an effort to challenge and/or manage fear, we must separate ourselves from fear."

fear, we must separate ourselves from fear. You are not fear. You can't be fear and made in God's image.

For this purpose, there is another exercise for you. Now, you definitely have to keep an open mind with this one. The goal of this exercise is to assist you in learning how to challenge or manage your fear. In an effort to do this, you are going to personify fear. What does that mean? I want you to visualize what fear looks like to you. It's hard to challenge and/or manage something that you can't see, touch, feel, or smell, right? So, this exercise is designed to help you with that so that it can be a little easier for you to challenge and/or manage your fear.

> "Visualize what fear looks like to you."

Exercise 3:

Close your eyes and reflect on your fear. If you had to give it an image or form, what would it look like? What color would it be? Now, open your eyes and draw that image in the area below. Don't worry about the fact that you may not be an artist. This is just for you!

Fear: _____

Take a look at your picture. Now that you have given it an image/form, go ahead and name your fear right above your picture.

Exercise 4:

Now that you have named and provided an image/form to your fear. Where is it in proximity to you? Draw where and how you see yourself in relationship with fear. How does that relationship look to you?

Fear: _____

Examine this picture. What do you think about it? Looking at this picture, how does it make you feel? What do you notice about it? Is your fear attractive or unattractive? Is your fear big or small? Is there room for you to move around it? If not, what does that mean? What is the true purpose of fear for you?

If it is blocking you in all areas, then fear has you where it wants you. It has you stuck, unable to fully grow and recognize your purpose. If it is so big that you can't even see around it, over it, or through it, then it has blocked your vision. Sometimes, we give fear so much power and authority over our lives that we can't see, hear, or move. If you have no vision, you are lost. In our relationship with God, there is purpose for our lives. If we can't hear Him or refuse to hear Him due to fear, then how can God direct us? If we can't move or refuse to move out of fear, then how can we walk into our full potential?

We forget that God made us in His image, and He did not create in us a spirit of fear. God is not fear. God is not confusion. God is not chaos. When we begin to experience these feelings in the midst of our storm, it's not because we did something wrong. The enemy comes to steal, kill, and destroy. When the enemy has done that, things tend to calm down and become really easy because he has done what he came to do. The enemy has stolen something from you, such as your self-image, your joy, your heart, your mind, or whatever he set out to take.

He stole it in an effort to have you question God and to cause a division in your relationship with God. When you begin to separate yourself from your fear (the enemy), you begin to take back that power and move towards activating your purpose.

ANGER

"My dear brothers and sisters, take note of this:
Everyone should be quick to listen, slow to speak and
slow to become angry, because human anger does not
produce the righteousness that God desires."

James 1: 19 – 20 (NIV)

Y ou may ask where anger comes into play regarding fear. Well, anger enters into the picture when you start fighting the person you are destined to be in life. Sometimes the plans we have for our lives don't align with God's plan for our lives. Due to God granting us free will, we proceed to follow our own direction. This is the issue with that. God has instilled specific talents and skills within us to fulfill His purpose for our lives. However, we may ignore the talents and skills that we have been blessed with because they do not align with our plans for our lives. Although we may have the intellect, talent, and skills to implement the plan we have developed for our lives, we may not be as good in that area due to the fact that it does not align with God's purpose. If we align ourselves with God's purpose, our thought processes, our talents, and our skill sets are exceptional. God gives us what we need to fulfill His purpose. Deep down, we know whether or not we are fulfilling our purpose. When we experience constant anger, irritability, or frustration, those are signs that we are not truly happy with where we are or who we are in life.

We experience anger as a result of various issues, such as people cutting us off on the road, failing a test at school, irritating customers at work, a diagnosis of cancer, outstanding bills, and many others. We often become angry and frustrated with a variety of people, such as parents, spouses, children, family, friends, colleagues, supervisors, and the list goes on and on. Is it wrong to be angry?

It depends on your perspective on anger. Your anger can be a motivator or a hindrance to your life. If you look at anger as motivation to strive to do better in life or to push you to another level, then that is a healthy form of anger. Take that failure, use what you have learned through that experience, and push through towards a more positive outlook for yourself in the future. However, anger is considered to be negative if one allows their anger to consume them. If your anger is leading you to engage in physical/verbal altercations, you have allowed your anger to take over. This form of anger can only hinder you from reaching your own goals and fulfilling God's potential for your life.

People often struggle with managing their anger in appropriate ways. Some people externalize their anger by engaging in arguments with others, engaging in physical fights with others, throwing objects within proximity, and tearing up papers. Some people may turn their anger, or any other emotion that they may be feeling, onto themselves. This is where you start to see behaviors, such as low self-esteem, symptoms of depression/anxiety, and self-injurious behaviors (i.e. cutting, burning, self-medicating, etc.). This is the most dangerous form of anger. No one can read your mind. Therefore, no one knows the negative messages that you feed yourself on a daily basis as a result of life stressors. Whether or not we engage in physical/verbal altercations or keep all of our emotions inside, our anger is often misdirected.

Many times, we will direct or project our anger onto something or someone else in an effort to avoid addressing conflict with the person we are truly angry with at the time. Therefore, the issue is never really addressed and continues to fester in our lives. This can lead to failed friendships, failed relationships, a negative self-image, and an increase in medical and mental health issues. You may ask yourself how misdirected anger can lead to failure in your relationships. Well, would you stay with a person who constantly takes their anger out on you for something you did not do? How long will that relationship last? For those who internalize their anger, how long do you think it takes for one's self-image to be tarnished in one's eyes if they continuously

> "We will direct or project our anger onto something or someone else in an effort to avoid addressing conflict with the person we are truly angry with at the time."

engage in negative self-talk? When you continue to internalize your emotions without addressing the true issue, it will affect every area of your life.

Let's examine how anger impacts one's relationship with God as an example. When people are asked if they are angry with God, people seem to hesitate. Why is that? There is a certain fear or reluctance in acknowledging that one is angry with God. We have been taught that it is wrong and disrespectful to be angry with God. My question is, "Why?" If God is an omniscient, loving, forgiving, and compassionate God, can't He handle your anger with Him? I think this is something that you have to learn as you continue to develop and grow in your relationship with God. We look at God as the Alpha and the Omega (our Creator), not necessarily as our Father. There are many sides to God, just like there are many sides to us. After all, mankind was made in God's image. I think we often have this reverence for God but forget that our goal is also to develop a personal relationship with Him. God desires a personal relationship with us. If we have a personal relationship with God, then why is it so wrong and disrespectful to be angry with Him? When you think of your relationship with your parents, siblings, and other family members, don't you become angry and frustrated with them at times? It is inevitable and expected. Just because you are family

> "God desires a personal relationship with you."

does not mean that you will always agree. When we became upset with our parents when we were younger, what would they say to us (if you were not being disrespectful)? What's wrong? Tell me what's going on with you. Why are you so angry? Don't you think God yearns to have this conversation with us? So, He sits and waits for you to share your thoughts/feelings with Him? Can you address the issue if you refuse to acknowledge or even express your feelings? What happens when you do not address the anger? It festers within your spirit, and the anger slowly eats away at you until it consumes you. When you allow your anger to consume you, how likely are you to hear someone who tries to talk to you, comfort you, or provide you with guidance? Not likely. How can you resolve anything when you are closed off and refuse to listen? Here comes that misdirected anger that I talked about earlier. You can't be angry at God, so who receives your anger and frustration? It's better than saying to God, "You have some serious explaining to do." At some point, you have to address your anger with the correct person in an effort to address it.

So, who are you really upset with when you think about it? After all, you have been given free will to make your own decisions. Often times, we are so focused on doing things our own way that we choose another path that does not lead us towards fulfilling our purpose. Deep down, we knew we were making the wrong choice. We saw some signs indicating that we needed to make a U-turn and choose another direction. However, we become so focused on what we want that we ignored who we really are and our true purpose. When we achieve what it is we think we wanted, then we realize that something is missing. When we look in the mirror, we realize that there is a void in our lives. We are not as happy as we would like to be due to this void. When we recognize that our "ideal" plan for our lives is not working out how we thought it would, we become upset and angry. Why are you angry? We achieved what we set out to achieve. However, there comes a moment in time when we realize that our "ideal" plan is not in alignment with our true purpose. We realize how much time has been wasted due to our stubbornness and the need to prove something to others. We realize that we have missed out on so many opportunities and blessings due to the fact that we chose to follow our own path. Sometimes, it's hard to take ownership of our actions and to hold ourselves accountable. So, what do we do? We find someone else to blame. We project our anger onto others, such as your family, partners, friends, and God. At some point, we have to reflect back on the decisions that we made for our lives. Have these decisions enhanced your growth and development or hindered it? Only when we are able to be open and honest

> "Only when we are able to be open and honest with ourselves and acknowledge our mistakes can we move forward and focus on becoming our best selves."

with ourselves and acknowledge our mistakes can we move forward and focus on becoming our best selves and activating our purpose.

Envision
Your
Dream

VISION

"Write the vision, and make it plain upon tables, that he may run that readeth it. For the vision is yet for an appointed time, but at the end it shall speak, and not lie: though it tarry, wait for it; because it will surely come, it will not tarry."

Habakkuk 2: 2 – 3 (KJV)

W hen we are young, we are filled with so many hopes and dreams. Our parents would ask us, "What do you want to be?" And we would say things like "a princess," "a doctor," "an astronaut," "a police officer," and many others. We were encouraged to reach for our dreams. Can you remember what you dreamed of when you were younger? Take a minute. Write it in the cloud below.

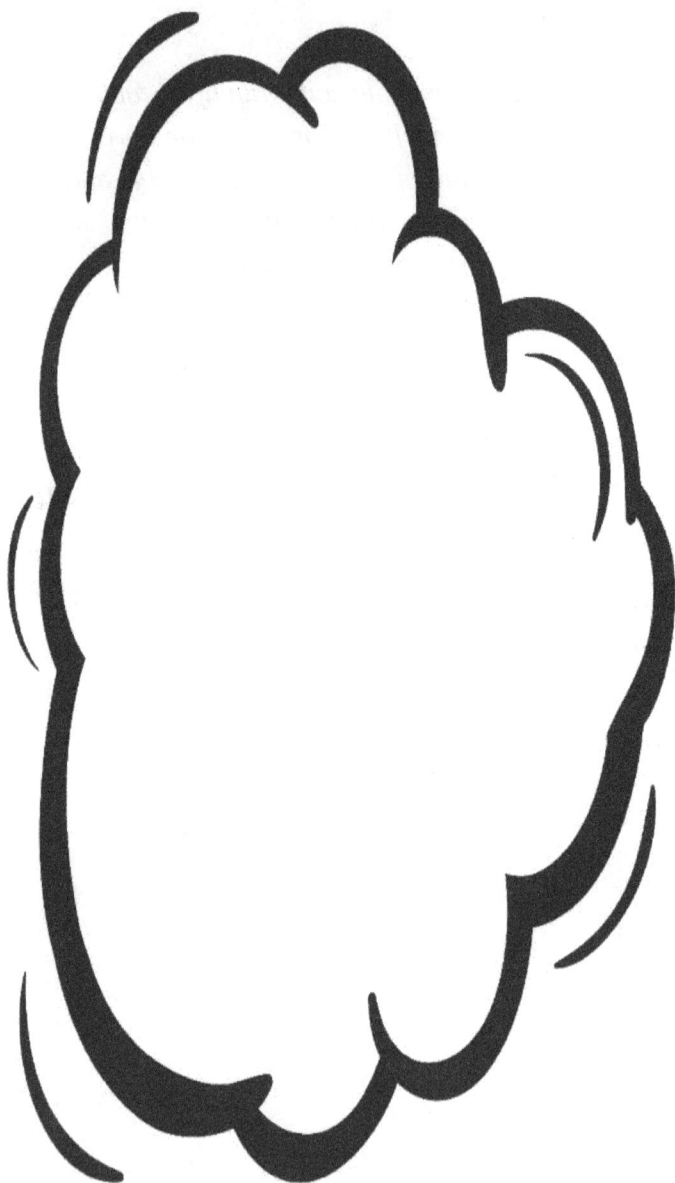

It's fun to look back on what your dreams were as a child. You didn't care about what others thought. You didn't care about how much schooling was needed or if you had the mental capacity for that profession. All you knew was what you wanted for your life. If you really take a look at your cloud, it provides you with a glimpse of your authentic self. Remember . . . this was YOU when you DARED to believe in yourself. This was YOU before you were introduced to fear and people who were discouraging of your dreams. As you reflect over what is written in your cloud, what do you see?

Try to look beyond the words. For example, . . . If doctor is written in your cloud, what traits do you associate with a doctor? Maybe, you are compassionate, have a desire to help others, or are empathetic. If a firefighter was written in your cloud, what do you see? Maybe, you are a risk-taker, have a desire to protect others, a desire to help others, or you are a good problem solver.

Exercise 4: Write 5 Character Traits that you see in your cloud.

1. _____

2. _____

3. _____

4. _____

5. _____

As you look at the five traits written above, what appeals to you about this list of traits? Do you feel that you possess all of these traits? Or . . . are there some traits that you didn't realize you possessed because they have been hidden or buried for so long? Now that you have taken a trip down memory lane, let's focus your attention on the present. You still have dreams! Where are you in achieving those dreams? Have you discarded your dreams? Have you told yourself that you don't have what it takes to achieve your dreams? Have you allowed people to discourage you from pursuing your dreams? Well, it's time you gave yourself permission to dream. Let your imagination run wild. Don't worry about how you are going to achieve your dream or what others are going to say or think. This is for you. If you can't visualize your dream, then how can you work towards achieving it? So, take a moment and write down what your dreams are today in the cloud below.

> "You still have dreams!"

When you write your dreams down and make them plain, it does something to your mindset. Think about it. What is more real to you . . . something that you envision in your head or something written down on paper? It's harder to believe in or manage something that you can't see. Therefore, it's easier for your vision or dream to get lost if it remains a thought in your head. Let's face it, how many thoughts run through your head every day? How many of those thoughts do you actually follow through with during the day? So if you feel as

"When you have a vision or a dream, be intentional with the way you handle it."

though you have a vision or a dream for yourself, be intentional with the way you handle it. You already encounter various afflictions, fears, and discouraging people that will assist in tearing down your dreams. Do you really want to be a part of that too?

Dare
To Be
Your
Authentic
Self

SELF-EMPOWERMENT

"Therefore, we do not lose heart. Though outwardly we are wasting away, yet inwardly we are being renewed day by day. For our light and momentary troubles are achieving for us an eternal glory that far outweighs them all. So, we fix our eyes not on what is seen, but on what is unseen, since what is seen is temporary, but what is unseen is eternal."

2 Corinthians 4:16 – 18 (NIV)

I f I asked you on a scale of 1 (extremely negative) – 10 (extremely positive) how you feel about yourself, what would you rate yourself? What do you like about yourself, and what do you not like about yourself? Your self-image is shaped by countless experiences throughout your life. As a result of some of your past experiences, you learned a number of life lessons. You learned how it felt to be hurt and rejected by family, friends, colleagues, and acquaintances. Being hurt and rejected by others never feels good.

> "Walls are built as a defense mechanism to avoid feeling hurt and rejected."

Therefore, walls are built as a defense mechanism to avoid feeling hurt and rejected again. You learn how to hide behind those walls and bury certain parts of yourself in an effort to feel accepted. However, there is one person who is not fooled by the person you're pretending to be. It's **YOU!** Have you ever wondered why you are never truly happy with yourself? There comes a point in time when you get tired of pretending. What happens when the walls you built no longer apply to your current situation? Those walls are no longer your shield of protection but a hindrance to you. They are now blocking you from being your authentic self and achieving your desired goals. Think about what the walls represent for you. Maybe the walls represent your distrust of others, fear of failure, fear of starting your own business, or fear of pursuing a relationship that you have always wanted. Does the existence of these walls set the tone for your success? Not likely. Therefore, an internal battle within yourself is activated.

> "There is one person who is not fooled by the person you're pretending to be. It's You!"

You are battling against the person that you are today versus the person that you are destined to be (your authentic self). This is where you have to revisit your relationship with the walls that you have built. You have to decide whether or not your relationship with your walls is healthy or unhealthy. Are you willing to live a life where you don't reach your full potential for fear of challenging and tearing down your walls? If you're willing to remain in the same place and never reach your full potential, then that is totally your decision. If you are looking for more, then I challenge you to ring the alarm and do something different. I want you to reflect on what you have already read because we are going to start putting it together like a puzzle. In the beginning, we discussed identifying your affliction and determining the factor(s) that may be holding you back. Second, we examined your fear(s) and your relationship with your fear(s). Upon completion of those exercises, you were able to determine whether or not you had a healthy or unhealthy relationship with your fear(s). Third, you reflected on what you really want for yourself in this life. If you were really honest with yourself, you might have discovered some things/traits about yourself that you hid or kept buried from others in an effort to avoid being hurt or rejected. Now it's time to put all of this together to determine how you are going to get out of your own way and activate your authentic self.

Take a minute and examine the following diagram. What comes to mind as you look at this diagram?

The Loop of Affliction

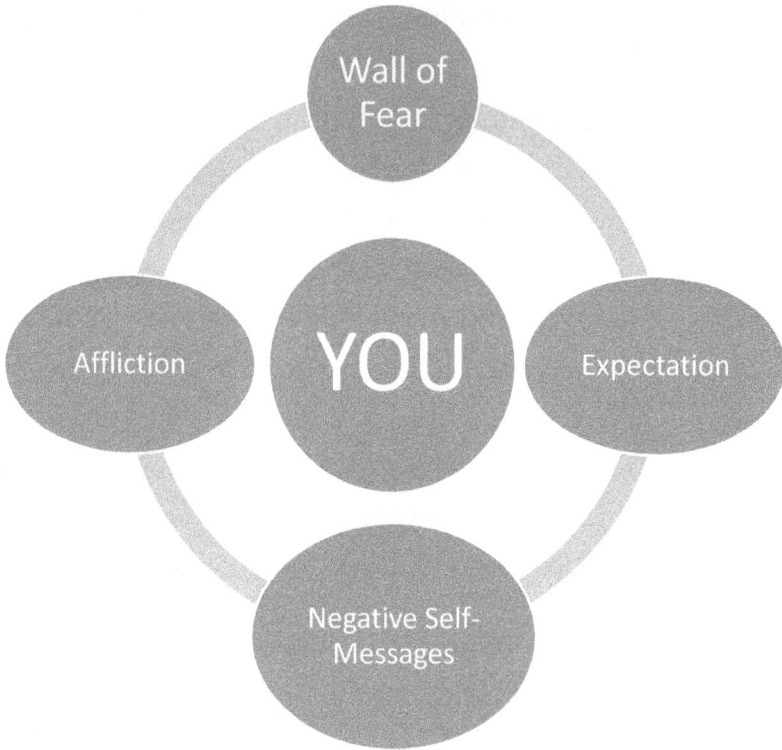

What does the Loop of Affliction mean to you? I introduced this concept because being stuck in your own head can be like a vicious cycle. If you allow what hinders you (the affliction) to take over and consume you, then you get caught in the loop. For example, your affliction may be that you suffer from low self-esteem. The reason you may be suffering from low self-esteem is due to being bullied or teased throughout your life.

Therefore, you build this wall (a shield of protection) to prevent you from being hurt or rejected in the future. However, you have an expectation of one day having close and intimate connections with others. Yet, the wall that you built to protect yourself from being hurt or rejected also hinders you from being vulnerable and trusting of others. Therefore, there's a struggle to meet your expectation because the wall acts as a barrier versus a shield of protection. This prompts the negative self-messages that you may feed yourself, such as "I'm not good enough," "I'm not smart enough," and "I'm not pretty enough." The negative self-talk reinforces your low self-esteem. You continue to loop through The Loop of Affliction. Make sense? Okay, so what's the next step?

Let's take a look at your relationship with the wall. What do you notice about the picture below?

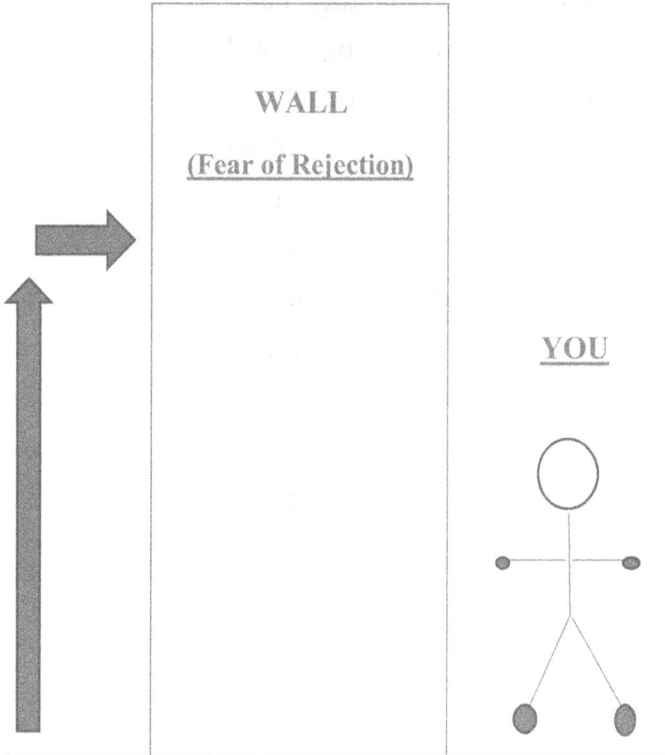

CODE R.E.D.

WALL

(Fear of Rejection)

YOU

HAPPINESS   POSITIVE SELF-IMAGE
ACCEPTANCE   INTIMATE RELATIONSHIPS

Notice the size of the wall compared to you. Notice the thickness of this wall. Remember that you built this wall to be a shield of protection for you? Take a good look at your wall. Can you get over the wall? Can you go under the wall? Can you go through the wall? Can you see what's on the other side of the wall? If the responses to the above questions were, "No," then what does this mean? It's time to change your perspective on the way you view your wall. You may need a notebook or a journal to start writing this down. In order to do this, we need to personify your relationship with the wall. In the Fear chapter, do you remember reflecting on your relationship with fear? This is what needs to happen here with your wall. Therefore, go ahead and name your wall. It could be anything that you want to call it. Determine whether or not you have a healthy or unhealthy relationship with your wall by identifying why you consider the relationship unhealthy and the benefits of remaining in relationship with the wall. Write this down on your wall.

DARKNESS

Why is Darkness unhealthy?

1. No friends
2. Distrust of others
3. Inability to be vulnerable
4. Feels sad
5. Lonely

Benefits

1. Know what to expect
2. Avoid getting hurt

YOU

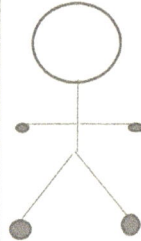

| HAPPINESS | POSITIVE SELF-IMAGE |
| ACCEPTANCE | INTIMATE RELATIONSHIPS |

So, I have determined that the relationship with Darkness is unhealthy based on the evaluation of the reasons this relationship is considered unhealthy versus the benefits of remaining in this relationship. So, what's the next step?

Think about the dynamics of an unhealthy relationship. In an unhealthy relationship, there is usually one person who holds the majority of the power, authority, and influence over the other person. Now, the relationship seems to be going well for that person. So, that person does not want this relationship to end. Therefore, that person will do or say things to the other person in an effort to manipulate him/her into staying in the unhealthy relationship. Now, I want you to think about what your wall says to you in an effort to manipulate you into remaining in this unhealthy relationship. Be honest with yourself. This exercise is not meant to be easy. When a person tries to manipulate you into remaining in an unhealthy relationship, that person does not play fair. So, write down those negative statements made to you by the wall.

Your picture should now look like this.

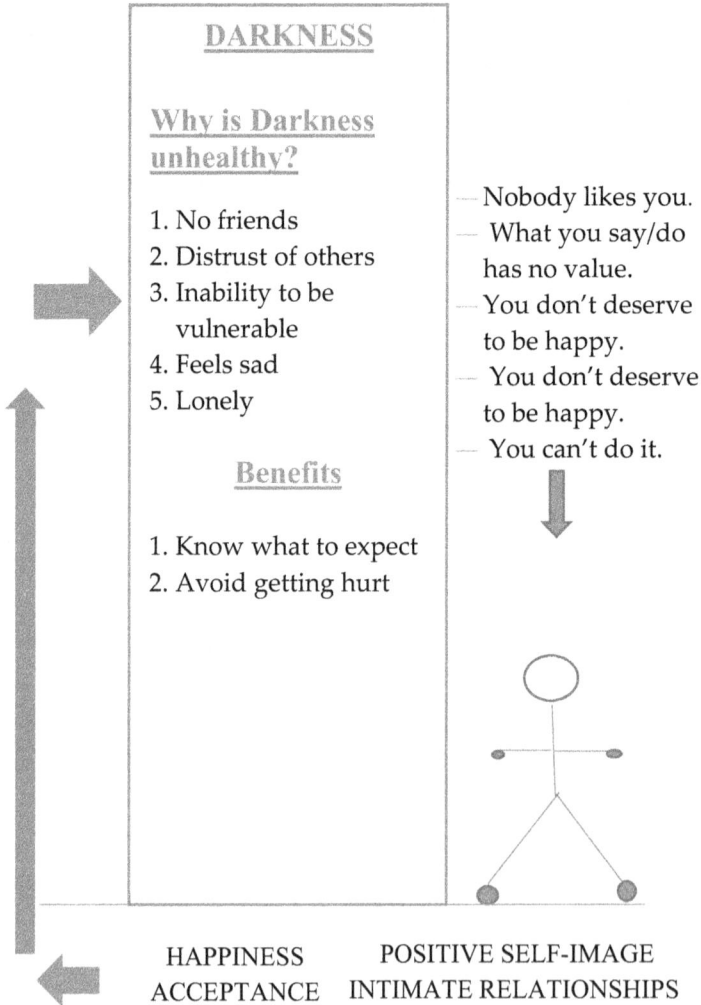

DARKNESS

Why is Darkness unhealthy?

1. No friends
2. Distrust of others
3. Inability to be vulnerable
4. Feels sad
5. Lonely

Benefits

1. Know what to expect
2. Avoid getting hurt

— Nobody likes you.
— What you say/do has no value.
— You don't deserve to be happy.
— You don't deserve to be happy.
— You can't do it.

HAPPINESS   POSITIVE SELF-IMAGE
ACCEPTANCE   INTIMATE RELATIONSHIPS

When you look at the picture above, how do you feel about it? Does it make you feel good about where you are in life? If it doesn't, what do you plan to do about it? I dare you to choose you. I dare you to be your true, authentic self. I dare you to be the person you were destined to be and walk into your purpose. If you accept the dare, I will share with you how to tear down your wall. Are you ready? This is the secret to tearing down the wall. You created the wall. Therefore, you have the power to tear down the wall. Now you may be asking, "How do I do that?" Well, you have to start challenging all of the negative messages that the wall feeds you on a daily basis. What do I mean by that? For every negative message the wall feeds you, you must challenge and counter that statement with three to five statements of your own. For years, the wall has been feeding you these negative statements. As a result of being fed these negative statements for years, you begin to believe them. Therefore, the goal is to challenge those statements until you no longer believe them. Every time you challenge those negative statements, you chip away at the wall. You chip away at the wall until the result of your chipping away at your wall becomes holes. As you continue to challenge these negative statements, those holes become bigger until the wall begins to crumble.

> "You have the power and authority to tear down the wall."

Your picture should now look like this.

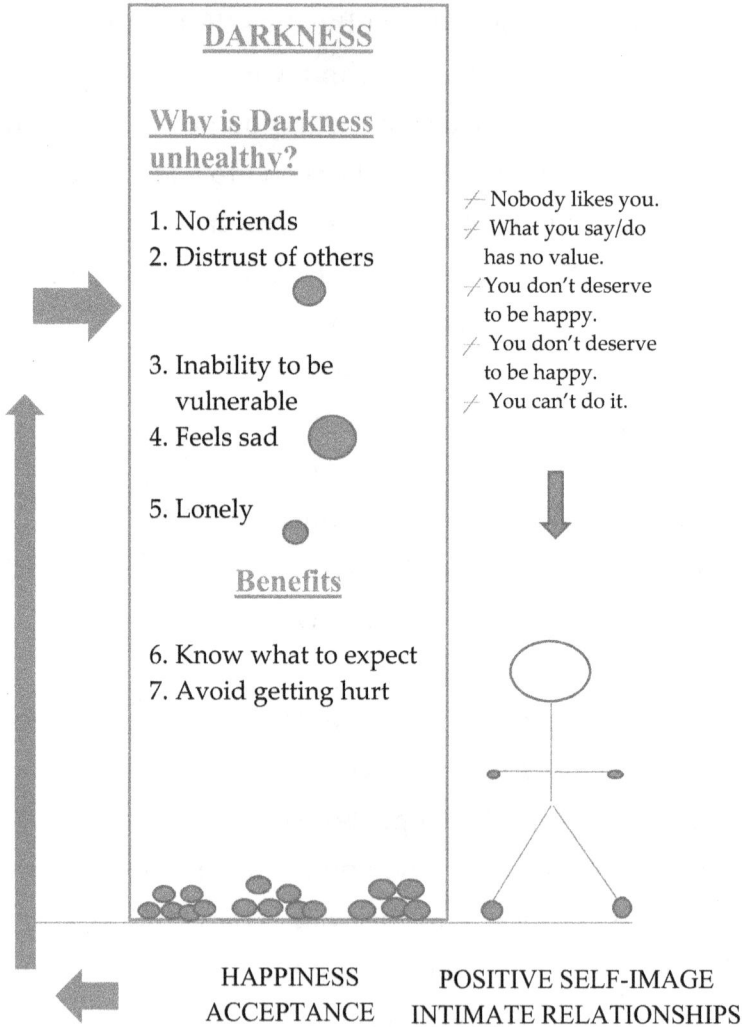

DARKNESS

Why is Darkness unhealthy?

1. No friends
2. Distrust of others

3. Inability to be vulnerable
4. Feels sad

5. Lonely

Benefits

6. Know what to expect
7. Avoid getting hurt

- Nobody likes you.
- What you say/do has no value.
- You don't deserve to be happy.
- You don't deserve to be happy.
- You can't do it.

HAPPINESS POSITIVE SELF-IMAGE
ACCEPTANCE INTIMATE RELATIONSHIPS

Take a look at the picture above. This is your strategy . . . your action plan. Think about it. When you go to war, you don't enter into the battlefield blind. You must have a strategy or action plan for victory. It's time to go to war . . . Ring the Alarm!!! Every time those negative statements come up, write them down so that you can challenge them. You must be consistent though. Eventually, those negative statements will start to come up less and less. In the process of challenging these negative statements, you are building up your self-confidence, reassuring yourself of who you really are, and fulfilling the need within yourself rather than remaining in an unhealthy relationship that you think is fulfilling your needs. Once you sever the ties (the negative statements) with your wall, you have succeeded in tearing down the wall.

With the wall torn down, your picture should now look like this.

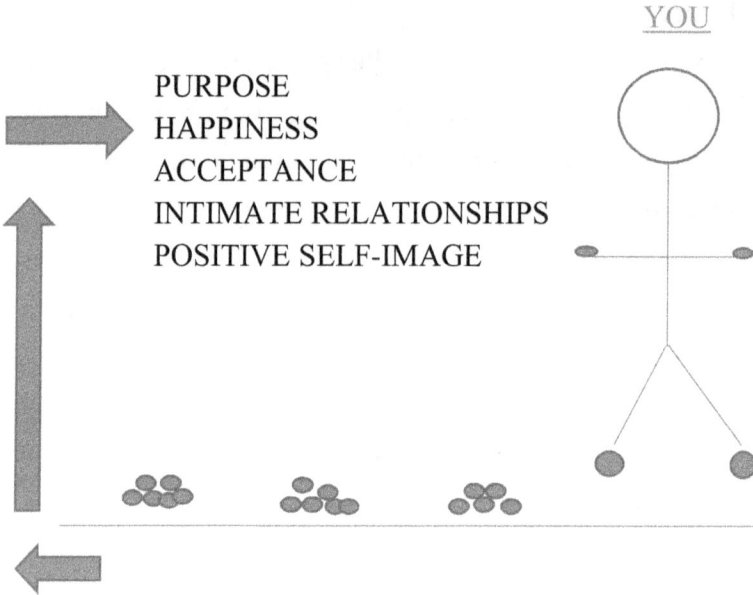

What do you notice about the above picture now that the wall has been torn down? In examining the picture, your vision for what you want for yourself and your life is now visible to you. Now that the wall is no longer hindering you from your vision, you have the ability to access your dreams, your goals, and your purpose. This is not to say that the path to your dreams, goals, and purpose is a smooth one, but you can see the light at the end of the tunnel. In order to make your dreams, your goals, and your purpose a reality, you must first be able to visualize it. Based on this picture, you are well on your way!

"In order to make your dreams, goals, and purpose a reality, you must first be able to visualize it."

Take a look at the image of you. What is the difference between the image of you in this picture and the image of you in the previous picture? The image of you in this picture is much larger due to the fact that you have taken back your power, your authority, and the influence that the wall had over you in that unhealthy relationship. The tearing down of the wall also symbolizes your willingness to take off the mask of the person that you have been pretending to be to reach for, and accept, your true, authentic self (the person that you were destined to be in this life). This is the beginning of your healing process.

HEALING

"He healeth the broken in heart,
and bindeth up their wounds."

Psalms 147:3 (KJV)

H ealing is a rough process for so many because it focuses so much on your inner self. It requires you to do a lot of self-examination and self-reflection. Self-reflection is not easy. If it was, everyone would do it and recognize the role they play in their own healing. As you maneuver through your journey called life, you were affected and influenced by many of your experiences. While some of the experiences created moments of happiness, moments of love, and moments of excitement, some of your experiences created moments of sadness, moments of hurt and pain, and moments of unacceptance. As a result, those experiences shaped you in a variety of ways. However, there are negative past experiences that we tend to hold onto in our lives. Some use those negative experiences as a motivator to propel them forward. Unfortunately, there are some that hold onto those negative experiences like they are a crutch. Those negative experiences are then utilized as a rationale for not moving forward with being one's authentic self or reaching for one's dreams. When you refuse to address or release past, negative experiences, it becomes a weight. Over time, the weight becomes heavier and heavier until it begins to take its toll on your mind, your body, and your emotional state. You begin to act as though you are still living in the past rather than living in the present. There are certain people you won't go around because you feel inferior to them. There are jobs you won't apply for due to the fact that you applied for a job in the past and did not receive the position. Maybe you lived through a bad break up in the past, and you refuse to become close to anyone in the present for fear of another broken heart. Take some time and reflect on the negative experiences that act as a hindrance or a barrier to your happiness or the fulfillment of your purpose. See . . . you may focus on the past so much that you have a hard time living in the present. As a result, you miss out on getting to know people or opportunities that were placed in your path to assist you with your healing, becoming your authentic self, and fulfilling your purpose.

> "You may focus on the past so much that you have a hard time living in the present."

There are many factors that contribute to the healing process. A requirement for healing is forgiveness. This is nothing new. People always talk about being able to forgive others. However, they often leave out how to forgive **yourself**. This is **BIG**. You may be saying to yourself, "What do I have to forgive myself for?" Think about it. We often blame ourselves for things that happen in our lives. Why is that? This is for those who feel they need to have control over everything in their lives. Sometimes it's easier to take responsibility for something than to believe that you have no control over some things that occur in your life. If there is some sense of control, then you know what to expect and can plan for that. So, some of the things that we need to forgive ourselves for is taking responsibility for things we have no control over in the first place. Remember, you can't control other people and what they will or will not do. You can only control yourself and your reaction. Sometimes relinquishing control may just provide you with a sense of freedom you seek in your life.

> "If an expectation is unattainable, then the expectation is unrealistic."

Second, let's take a look at your expectations. Let me ask you this question? Who is your worst critic? The most frequent response to that question is: **You!** We are our own worst critic. We are always harder on ourselves than others. Therefore, we may need to forgive ourselves for not being perfect. Someone needs to hear this. If you're perfect, then you don't make any mistakes. Well, we all know that no one is perfect. So, is this a realistic or unrealistic expectation? If an expectation is unattainable, then the expectation is unrealistic. We tend to set ourselves up for failure at times due to setting unrealistic expectations. What should you take away from this? One, we need to make sure that the expectations we set for ourselves are realistic and attainable. Second, we need to start giving ourselves a break. Everyone will make mistakes throughout their lifetime. That's a given. So, it's time to stop blaming ourselves for not always getting it right.

Third, it's really important to forgive yourself for not being your true, authentic self. Remember . . . self-reflection is not easy. Ask yourself these questions. Were you honest with yourself as you went through the chapters of this book and completed the exercises? What have you discovered about yourself

> *"It's time to be vulnerable with the one person that matters right now. That's You!"*

as a result? It's time to be vulnerable with the one person that matters right now. That's **YOU!** It's time to have your own personal POW WOW session with yourself. This is your time to examine yourself. Are you truly happy with who you are and where you are in your life right now? What do you feel as though you're missing? What do you feel like you need to do in an effort to be true to who you really are? Recognizing who you are and accepting yourself for who you are is essential to the healing process. Due to the struggle that some people have with loving themselves and accepting themselves for who they are, they tend to rely on others for that validation. Therefore, we look to others to love us the way we want to be loved and accept us for who we are. Well, what happens when the people you depend on for that validation don't love you the way you want

> "Your validation of who you are must come from within you."

to be loved or accept you for who you are? Then, your self-confidence plummets because you were seeking validation from them versus yourself. The validation must come from within you! Once you're able to accept yourself for who you are, then you are free to move towards activating your purpose.

The following exercise will close out this chapter on healing. Take some time and write a letter to yourself. This letter should be a letter of forgiveness. It's time to give yourself permission to forgive **You**! Forgive yourself for the mistakes that you made in the past. Forgive yourself for the failed relationships in your life. Forgive yourself for the missed opportunities that could have moved you forward in your purpose. Forgive yourself for giving your power and authority over to others. Forgive yourself for not honoring and loving yourself for who you are. You can only be healed if you release what you have been holding onto for so long. You no longer have to hold on to that baggage. Let Go and Let God!

> "Forgive yourself for not honoring and loving yourself for who you are."

When God created us, He created us with a purpose. What does that mean? Let's examine the word Purpose.

"**P**" stands for **powerful**. There is power in your thoughts. There is power in your words. There is power in your actions. You are strong and have the power and authority to walk into your full potential.

"**U**" stands for **unique**. There is no other person like you. There is no one else that can fulfill your purpose the way God intended for you to fulfill it.

"**R**" stands for **release**. You can't move forward if you continue to live in the past. You have to let go of some of the things that you are holding onto because they are now a weight that is holding you back from activating your purpose.

"**P**" stands for **peace**. Once you are walking in your purpose, it doesn't mean that you won't experience any trials or tribulations. However, you will have a sense of peace with yourself due to the fact that you know you are walking in your purpose.

"**O**" stands for **overflow**. You are gifted with the talent and skills necessary to fulfill your purpose. Therefore, you will experience an overflow as you walk in your purpose.

"**S**" stands for **survivor**. Fulfilling God's purpose for your life means that you have been tried and tested, and you have come out victorious.

"**E**" stands for **empowered**. You have been empowered to be who God has destined you to be and to handle your purpose.

This is who you are destined to be: A **powerful** and **unique** man or woman, who has been **released** to find their **peace** and **overflow** through their journey as a **survivor,** who has been **empowered** to activate their purpose.

God knows us, the true us. He knows the person that we often hide from others. God knows our heart and our desires. How He sees us often varies from how we see ourselves. God knows what we are and are not capable of in regard to our potential. The battle that occurs within us is due to the struggle that we are having between the person we are presenting to

> *"Our purpose is connected to others."*

others versus the person we are destined to be. Our struggle with activating our purpose is due to some of the decisions we make in our lives. Since God granted us free will, we often make choices for our lives out of fear, our expectations or expectations that have been placed on us, or the fact that one choice is easier than the other. Remember that we cannot fulfill our purpose if we don't go through the preparation process. Our decision to allow our affliction(s) to consume us can derail us from the path needed to prepare us to develop and grow into the person who can handle God's purpose for our lives. Our purpose is connected to others. If we don't activate our purpose, those who are connected to us may be derailed from their path to purpose as a result. For example, we are linked together like a chain. What happens if one of the links in the chain breaks? Then, there is a missing piece in the chain. However, that does not have to be your story. What I love about God is that He does not give up on us even when we give up on ourselves. We have multiple opportunities to get it right. Now that you have participated in the CODE R.E.D. experience, it's time to Ring the Alarm and activate your purpose!

NOTE TO THE READER

Dear Reader:

First, I want to thank you for taking the time to read and participate in the CODE R.E.D. experience. I know that life can get busy, and you end up focusing on everything but yourself. With that in mind, you have to learn how to be intentional about focusing on yourself and living in the present. You have to be intentional about your own self-care because you are worth it. With that said, I hope you were able to take advantage of the opportunity to learn some things about yourself. For you, I pray that you were able to tear down some walls and take back your power. I hope that you took the time to forgive yourself and release some of the things that you have been holding onto for years. I pray that you were able to Ring the Alarm and activate your purpose!

Connected Through Purpose,

Dr. Knight

www.ingramcontent.com/pod-product-compliance
Lightning Source LLC
Chambersburg PA
CBHW022031090426
42739CB00006BA/378